James Monroe

James Monroe

Andrew Santella

AMERICA'S
5TH
PRESIDENT

Children's Press®
A Division of Scholastic Inc.
New York / Toronto / London / Auckland / Sydney
Mexico City / New Delhi / Hong Kong
Danbury, Connecticut

Library of Congress Cataloging-in-Publication Data

Santella, Andrew.
     James Monroe / by Andrew Santella.
        p. cm. — (Encyclopedia of presidents)
        Summary: The life and long political career of the fifth president of the
United States, whose Monroe Doctrine proclaimed opposition to further
European control in the western hemisphere.
Includes bibliographical references and index.
  ISBN 0-516-24200-8
  1. Monroe, James, 1758–1831—Juvenile literature. 2.Presidents—United
States—Biography—Juvenile literature. [1. Monroe, James, 1758–1831. 2.
Presidents.] I. Title. II. Series.
  E372 .S267 2003
  973.5′4′092—dc21

                                                        2002008800

CHILDREN'S PRESS and associated logos are trademarks and or registered
trademarks of Scholastic Library Publishing. SCHOLASTIC and associated
logos are trademarks and or registered trademarks of Scholastic Inc.
1 2 3 4 5 6 7 8 9 10 R 12 11 10 09 08 07 06 05 04 03

Contents

Chapter 1

Making a Choice ———————————————

All across Virginia, people were choosing sides. The year was 1775. The long-running argument about whether Great Britain had the right to tax its American colonies was turning violent. Some Virginians were rushing to join patriot militias, which were preparing to fight the British. For the patriots, outright rebellion was the only answer to the harsh policies of the British government. Other Virginians remained loyal to the British. To them, the so-called patriots were simply traitors.

On June 24, 1775, a teenager named James Monroe made his choice. Monroe, a student at the College of William and Mary, joined a group of 24 patriots in a raid on the mansion of the British governor of Virginia, Lord Dunmore. At 17, Monroe was the youngest member of the raiding party. The raiders knew that Dunmore would not be at his mansion. Fearing for his safety, he had gone to live aboard a British warship off the coast of Virginia, leaving his servants to guard his home. The raiding party knew, however, that inside the mansion was a supply of muskets and swords. They wanted these weapons for the poorly armed patriot militia.

Monroe and the other patriots forced their way into the governor's mansion. The weapons were on display in the entry hall, serving as an exhibit of the military power of the British Empire. The raiders gathered 200 muskets and more than 300 swords and made their escape. Now the weapons could be used against the powerful British.

James Monroe's decision to join the raid on Lord Dunmore's mansion was probably the biggest one of his young life. Once he made it, there was no turning back. He was now committed to the patriot cause—a cause that made him a traitor in the eyes of some.

Monroe never wavered from that cause. He went on to fight with George Washington's army in the Revolutionary War. He served the young United States as a senator, as a diplomat, and as secretary of state. In 1817, he became the fifth president of the United States. By then, more than 40 years had passed, but he was still committed to the principles of the American Revolution. As president, Monroe led the United States into a new era, marked by westward expansion and a more prominent place among the nations of the world. His commitment to independence and self-government guided him as president just as they had when he was a young man in the first days of the Revolution.

The governor's mansion in Williamsburg, where Monroe and others took weapons for use by patriot militias.

Virginia Childhood ——————————————

James Monroe was born in Westmoreland County, Virginia, on April 28, 1758. He was the oldest son of Spence Monroe and Elizabeth Jones Monroe. James's father was a farmer who was active in Virginia politics. He raised tobacco and other crops on 500 acres (200 ha) of land in Westmoreland County, which stretches along the shore of the Potomac River, near where it enters Chesapeake Bay.

For Virginians of the 1700s, wealth and power were measured in land. In Virginia, only landowners had the right to vote and to serve on juries. As the owner of 500 acres, Spence Monroe was wealthy enough to be considered a respectable gentleman. However, he was nowhere near as wealthy as some of his neighbors. For example, the family of George Washington owned some 6,000 acres (2,400 ha), and other wealthy neighbors lived in huge mansions. The Monroe home was large and comfortable, but simple. Spence Monroe may have built the two-story house himself.

As the oldest son of the family, James knew that one day he would inherit all his father's land. Spence Monroe would teach James many of the skills he would need to manage a farm in the style of a Virginia gentleman. James probably learned from his father how to ride a horse and how to hunt for game for the family table.

A sketch of the house where Monroe was born in Westmoreland County, Virginia. It was torn down in the mid-1800s.

James also would have learned about Virginia's politics from his father. During his childhood, relations between Britain and her American colonies were becoming strained. Spence Monroe helped organize a written protest against British taxes in 1766, when James was eight years old.

Historians don't know much about James's mother, Elizabeth Jones Monroe. James described her simply as "a very amiable and respectable woman" and as "a good parent." She may have taught him to read and write and introduced him to arithmetic. He may have received further lessons from a tutor who visited him at home.

School Years

James did not attend a regular school until he was eleven. His father enrolled him in the Campbelltown Academy, a school run by the Reverend Archibald Campbell. It was a small school, with only 25 students, but it was considered one of the best in Virginia. Some of James's new classmates at Campbelltown were boarding students—they lived at the school or with local families during the school year. The Monroes' home was close enough to the school that James could live at home with his family. According to one story, he liked to carry his hunting rifle along on the long walk to school in case he had a chance to shoot a rabbit or squirrel along the way. James proved to be a good student. He excelled in Latin and mathematics.

James's teenage years were interrupted by tragedy. His mother died of unknown causes. Then, when he was 16, his father died. By this time, his older sister Elizabeth was married. He and his brothers went to live with their uncle, Judge Joseph Jones, and his family. Jones took an active role in raising James and his brothers. He was one of the leading political figures of Virginia and a member

"Silver Heels"

One of James Monroe's best friends at the Campbelltown Academy was John Marshall. He and James remained friends most of their lives. Like Monroe, Marshall was destined to become a national political leader. Marshall became chief justice of the United States, serving from 1801 until 1835. As a boy, however, Marshall was known for other talents. He was called "Silver Heels," because he was seldom beaten in foot races or high-jump contests.

John Marshall, Monroe's schoolmate, who later served as chief justice of the U.S. Supreme Court. When Monroe became president, Marshall administered the oath of office.

☆ ★ ☆

of the House of Burgesses, the assembly of representatives in colonial Virginia. Jones was a friend of George Washington and other colonial leaders.

James had nearly finished his studies at Campbelltown Academy, and Jones urged him to enroll in college. With Jones's help, James entered the College of William and Mary in Williamsburg. He was 16 years old—not an unusual age for college study then. Williamsburg was about 60 miles (100km) from Westmoreland County, so he would be living away from home for the first time.

Williamsburg

James moved into student rooms in the large brick building that housed the college. His new home was very different from the quiet farm he had left behind. Williamsburg was called the "chief city of the colony." Fine town houses and large shade trees lined the main boulevard, Duke of Gloucester Street. Fancy carriages pulled by matching teams of horses carried the wealthy of Williamsburg to the theater and to dress balls, or dances. Williamsburg was also the home of the colonial governor, and the place where Virginia lawmakers gathered once a year. It was the center of political life in Virginia.

Attending the College of William and Mary gave James his first close look at the world of politics. He could listen to people arguing about politics in

An early view of the College of William and Mary. The Wren Building (with spire) is still a part of the William and Mary campus.

the local taverns. He could attend the debates between leading political figures, who included Thomas Jefferson and Patrick Henry. At around this time, one observer wrote, "The reigning spirit in Virginia is liberty—and the universal topic [is] politics."

James arrived in Williamsburg just as the American Revolution was breaking out. For years, Britain's American colonies had protested the taxes and harsh laws imposed by Britain. In 1774, Virginia's House of Burgesses had asked the other colonies to send representatives to a meeting in Philadelphia to plan a unified response to Britain. The meeting became known as the First Continental Congress, and Virginia's representatives included George Washington, Patrick Henry, and James's uncle, Joseph Jones.

The British were acting, too. Virginia's British governor, Lord Dunmore, seized gunpowder belonging to the Williamsburg *militia* in April 1775. (Just a day earlier, British troops on similar missions in Massachusetts fought with militia in Lexington and Concord in the first important battles of the Revolutionary War.) In response, some students at the college began forming militia units and drilling with weapons. James bought a rifle and took part in the drills. In June, he took part in the raid on Lord Dunmore's mansion, the first of his actions in support of the patriot cause.

Chapter 2

Joining the Fight ——————————

With a revolution breaking out around him, Monroe must have found it difficult to concentrate on his studies. In the spring of 1776, he decided that the cause of the colonies was more important than college. He and his college roommate, John Mercer, enlisted in the Continental Army, and were made lieutenants in the Third Virginia Infantry. After a few months of training, they marched off with the regiment to join George Washington's Continental Army, which was under attack by the British in New York City.

Monroe's regiment joined the fight on September 16 as Washington's troops were in retreat from New York City. The Virginians helped set up a counterattack against the British, which drove them back nearly a mile. This battle of Harlem Heights was a rare victory in a string of discouraging defeats for the Americans. As winter approached, they

were driven out of New York altogether and continued to retreat westward across New Jersey and into Pennsylvania. Morale was low, and illness and desertions sapped the strength of Washington's army.

Washington badly needed a victory. He planned a surprise attack on a British

In the Battle of Harlem Heights, Continental Army soldiers (right) attack the British (center) and force them to retreat.

garrison in Trenton, New Jersey, which was manned by 1,500 Hessians, troops from the state of Hesse in present-day Germany, who had been hired and paid by the British.

On Christmas Day, 1776, Washington posted guards on the road to Trenton to keep it clear of Hessian scouts. Monroe was part of a unit assigned to this important patrol. Then, Monroe's unit joined the 2,400 other troops who crossed the icy Delaware River into New Jersey in the middle of the night.

When the Continentals charged the following morning, Monroe's unit was in the lead. The Hessians, recovering from their Christmas celebrations the night before, hurriedly tried to set up a cannon to fire on the attackers. Monroe led a charge that captured the cannon, but during the fighting, he was badly wounded in the shoulder, becoming one of the few American casualties. The attackers captured or killed more than 1,000 Hessians in a stunning victory.

Monroe received a commendation for his bravery, and was promoted to captain. However, he remained out of action for three months while he recovered from his wound. When he was well enough to go home, Monroe was assigned to recruit soldiers in Virginia for the Continental Army. This was a discouraging job because many able-bodied young men were already serving in the Continental Army or the Virginia militia. Others were not interested in the difficult life of a Continental soldier.

Returning to Washington's army, Monroe became an aide to General William Alexander, also known as Lord Stirling. (Although born in the American colonies, Lord Stirling claimed the title of a Scottish earldom.) As an aide to Lord Stirling, Monroe handled a great deal of paperwork. He wrote out letters that the general dictated and made endless copies of battle orders to be sent to other officers. Other parts of the job were more exciting. Monroe participated in meetings to plan campaigns and battles. Serving at the general's side, he learned much about how an army operates. He also made lasting friendships with officers from other colonies and even from Europe—men who had come to the new United States to help in the fight for independence.

During 1777, a British army from New York attacked in Pennsylvania and captured the city of Philadelphia. The Continental Congress, which met in Philadelphia, was driven out of the city. Washington's army retreated to winter quarters at Valley Forge, Pennsylvania. Monroe spent that miserable winter with the army. With few supplies, inadequate clothing, and little food, morale was low.

Baron von Steuben (right) drills American soldiers in the bitter cold at Valley Forge early in 1778.

Among the men serving under Washington at Valley Forge were several Europeans lending their services to the American cause. They had little in common except their commitment to liberty and their very long names. Marie-Joseph-Paul-Yves-Roch-Gilbert du Motier, Marquis de Lafayette (1757–1834) was a young French nobleman and soldier who came in 1777 to fight in the Revolution. He became a close friend of Washington, and served under him for the rest of the war.

Friedrich Wilhelm Ludolf Gerhard Augustin von Steuben (1730–1794) was an experienced officer in the Prussian army (Prussia is part of present-day Germany). Early in 1778, von Steuben began drilling the Continental Army, turning it into a more disciplined fighting force.

The Marquis de Lafayette, a young French nobleman, came to America to fight for American independence and served as an officer under George Washington.

One of Monroe's close friends was Pierre Stephen DuPonceau, another young Frenchman who served as an aide to von Steuben. DuPonceau and Monroe lent each other their favorite books and spent hours around the campfire discussing philosophy and politics.

☆ ★ ☆

The soldiers built crude log huts, filling the gaps with mud plaster to offer some little protection from snow and cold. Hunger and illness were constant problems. Some men had no shoes. They tied rags around their feet instead—not much help in the mud and snow of a Pennsylvania winter.

Still, Washington kept discipline in the camp. With the help of von Steuben and others, the Continental Army became a stronger fighting force. That summer, Monroe saw action at the Battle of Monmouth in New Jersey on June 28. He led a scouting party that brought back valuable information and helped save the Continentals from defeat.

Monroe grew more dissatisfied with his job as aide. He wanted to command troops in battle, but there were few command positions available. He returned to Virginia, hoping to gain a command in the state militia, but was unsuccessful there as well. He did meet Virginia governor Thomas Jefferson. Jefferson liked Monroe immediately and offered advice about his future, suggesting that he should prepare for a life in politics by studying law. Jefferson suggested law books to begin reading, and began introducing Monroe to other leaders in Virginia. In 1780, the Virginia capital was moved from Williamsburg to Richmond. Governor Jefferson moved to the new capital city, and Monroe followed. The two continued their friendship.

Entering Politics

In 1781, a British army under Lord Cornwallis surrendered to a combined American and French force at Yorktown, Virginia, a few miles from Williamsburg. The surrender was the last major military action in the war for independence, even though it was two years until the final peace treaty was signed. Monroe turned his attention from military matters to political matters. He wanted to play a part in the political life of the new nation.

In 1782, Monroe ran for and was elected to a seat in the Virginia House of Delegates, the lower house of the Virginia legislature. He so impressed his colleagues there that they appointed him to the Governor's Council, a group of eight advisers to the governor.

In June 1783, the legislators selected Monroe as one of Virginia's representatives to the Continental Congress. In November, when he took his seat with representatives from the former colonies, Congress was temporarily meeting in Annapolis, Maryland. Monroe shared rooms with Jefferson, who was also a Virginia representative.

During the recesses between Congress's sessions, Monroe traveled to learn more about the new United States. On one trip, he attended an Indian conference near Albany, New York, and visited Montreal in Canada. On a second trip, he crossed the Appalachian Mountains for the first time, visiting present-day

Kentucky. In the years ahead, Monroe would become a strong supporter for developing the lands west of the mountains.

In 1785, Congress began meeting in New York City. There, Monroe met Elizabeth Kortright, the daughter of a New York merchant. At 17, she was ten years younger than Monroe. She was considered one of New York's great beauties. They married on February 16, 1786, and spent a honeymoon on rural Long Island, outside the city. When Monroe's term in Congress ended in November, he and Eliza moved to Fredericksburg, Virginia. By the end of the year, they welcomed their first child. They named her Eliza, after her mother.

A miniature portrait of young Elizabeth Monroe, painted in the 1790s when she and her husband lived in Paris.

As a member of Congress, Monroe witnessed firsthand the challenges faced by the new U.S. government. Under the Articles of Confederation, there was no president. There were no federal courts. Congress had no power to raise money through taxation. In fact, Congress was so weak and ineffective that some members didn't bother to attend the sessions.

Clearly, change was needed. James Madison, another Virginian with close ties to Thomas Jefferson, was a leader in urging that the Articles of Confederation be changed or replaced. Finally, a convention of representatives from all the colonies gathered in Philadelphia in 1787. George Washington served as presiding officer. Madison and Alexander Hamilton of New York took leading roles in drafting a new document, which was called the Constitution. Delegates to the convention signed the Constitution in September 1787.

Before the Constitution could take effect, however, individual states had to *ratify*, or approve, it. At the Virginia ratifying convention, the debate was long and hard. Monroe agreed with Madison that a new plan of government was needed, but he believed that the Constitution as it was written did not protect the rights of individuals and gave too much power to the new federal government. He joined Patrick Henry and other Virginia leaders in opposing ratification. In the end, however, Madison's arguments for ratification won the day. The convention ratified the Constitution in 1789, becoming the tenth state to approve it.

The new government replaced the Continental Congress with a congress of two houses, the House of Representatives and the Senate. Monroe ran against James Madison for a seat in the new House of Representatives and lost. He soon got another chance to represent his state. In 1790, the Virginia legislature elected Monroe to become one of Virginia's two senators in the United States Senate.

The Birth of American Political Parties ——————

The first president, elected in 1789, was Virginia's own George Washington. He was elected by unanimous vote in the electoral college. There were no political parties to put up opposing candidates. It soon became clear, however, that there were major differences of opinion in the government. Monroe was part of a faction, or group, that believed that state governments and individual rights should not be weakened to make the new federal government stronger. This faction was led by Jefferson and Madison. Monroe quickly became one of its leaders in the Senate. The opposing faction favored a strong national government with broad powers to tax and regulate commerce. It was led by Vice President John Adams and Secretary of the Treasury Alexander Hamilton. Over the next few years, these factions organized themselves into the first American political parties. The Jefferson-Madison-Monroe party came to be known as Democratic-Republicans. The Adams-Hamilton party came to be known as Federalists.

Thomas Jefferson (above) and James Madison (opposite) were the main organizers of the Democratic-Republican Party. Monroe learned much from his fellow Virginians and held important posts when each served as president.

Democratic-Republicans and Federalists soon disagreed about other matters. In Europe, France was in the midst of a revolution, throwing off the rule of its king, Louis XVI, and trying to establish a new republic. When the revolution became violent, Great Britain began to prepare for war against the new French regime. The Democratic-Republicans supported France. They remembered the support of France during the American Revolution and believed the French Revolution carried on the values of the Americans' struggle to throw off the rule of a king. The Federalists favored Britain. They were horrified at the disorder in France and worried that a break with Britain would damage trade with the United States's most important trading partner.

When war between Britain and France began in 1792, President Washington was determined not to take sides. In 1794, he sent a Federalist, John Jay, to Britain to negotiate with the British, and he appointed Democratic-Republican James Monroe as minister to France. Monroe assured the French that the United States remained a friend. In the meantime, John Jay negotiated an important new commercial treaty with the British. The French were angry, asking how the United States could remain friends with both sides. They demanded to know what the treaty said. The treaty remained secret, and Monroe couldn't tell them.

A miniature portrait of James Monroe, painted when he was serving as minister to France in the 1790s.

Jay's Treaty, which gave great advantage to Britain in trading arrangements, was very unpopular in the United States. Even Washington and Hamilton were unhappy with some of the treaty, but they believed it was the only practical way to keep the United States out of a war that it was not strong enough to fight. Urged on by Hamilton, the Senate ratified the treaty.

When the French learned the terms of the treaty, they were angry, not only with the United States but also with Monroe. He had tried his best to keep the United States on friendly terms with France. Hamilton and the Federalists blamed him—not Jay's Treaty—for worsening relations with France. In 1796, Secretary of State Timothy Pickering persuaded President Washington to recall Monroe from France. With few friends in France and with enemies in the American government, Monroe sailed for home, angry and out of a job.

In Virginia, Monroe had bought a new estate in Albemarle County, not far from Jefferson's estate at Monticello. He and Eliza settled there. Monroe took up management of the new estate and participated in the political affairs of Virginia. He didn't forget the embarrassment of being fired by Washington. He wrote and published a book attacking the government's policies and defending his own actions. It was called *A View of the Conduct of the Executive in the Foreign Affairs of the United States Connected with the Mission to the French Republic During the Years 1794, 5 & 6.*

Monroe's Estates

Monroe's estate in Albemarle County was called Highland. The house he lived in with his family is still standing, and the estate, later renamed Ash Lawn, is now home to a museum, a working farm, and a performing arts festival.

☆ ☆ ☆

Monroe returned to politics in 1799, when he was elected governor of Virginia by the state legislature. The governor was given little power under the Virginia constitution, but Monroe tried to broaden the role of the governor in state politics. He was the first Virginia governor to give an annual address to the legislature, modeled on the president's address to Congress. In 1800, he led the state's efforts to put down a planned slave revolt. He served three one-year terms as governor.

In 1800, Thomas Jefferson ran for president against Federalist John Adams. The Democratic-Republicans were victorious, but Jefferson tied in electoral votes with his own vice-presidential candidate, Aaron Burr. In early 1801, the House of Representatives elected Jefferson, and the Democratic-Republicans took control of the government. In 1803, Jefferson called on his old friend Monroe to take on another mission to France.

By this time, France was ruled by the dictator Napoleon. He had arranged for Spain to cede the Louisiana Territory, a huge region west of the Mississippi River, to France. Jefferson was afraid that Napoleon might close the port of New Orleans at the mouth of the Mississippi to American trade or that he might even establish a French colony in the territory. He asked Monroe to go to France as a special envoy to help the minister to France, Robert R. Livingston, arrange for the United States to buy New Orleans. When Monroe arrived, he learned that Napoleon had offered to sell the whole Louisiana Territory or nothing at all.

Monroe and Livingston were in a difficult position. Napoleon wanted $15 million for the territory—a good price for such a huge region, but much more than they had permission to spend for New Orleans. There was no time to ask for further instructions—it would have taken months for messages to travel by ship twice across the Atlantic. The two Americans agreed to go ahead anyway, and they signed an agreement for the Louisiana Purchase.

Jefferson was pleased. The Democratic-Republican party led the fight in Congress to approve the purchase, and it became a new territory that nearly doubled the land area of the United States. Monroe won high praise for his role in arranging the Louisiana Purchase, and it brought him to national attention.

Monroe and Robert R. Livingston are completing negotiations with French foreign minister Talleyrand for the purchase of the Louisiana Territory in 1803. At the top corners are thumbnail portraits of U.S. President Thomas Jefferson and the French leader Napoleon.

The Louisiana Purchase

The Louisiana Purchase has been called the greatest real estate deal in history. For $15 million, the United States gained 828,000 square miles of territory between the Mississippi River and the Rocky Mountains. Today, the territory makes up all or part of thirteen states.

The limits of the Louisiana Purchase were vague at first. In this early map, it includes all of present-day Texas. However, Texas remained part of Spain's North American empire and did not become a part of the United States until 1845.

Monroe remained in Europe to take on a new assignment as minister to Great Britain, where he served from 1803 to 1807. Relations with Britain were tense and often unfriendly. Britain's trade policies discriminated against the United States. Worst of all, British warships stopped American merchant ships, searching them for deserters from the British navy. The British *impressed* those they suspected of being deserters—put them on British navy ships and forced them to serve as crewmen.

Monroe, with the help of another special envoy, worked long and hard to negotiate a new commercial treaty with Britain that would improve relations between the two countries. They gained some concessions, but the British would not agree to end impressment. He sent the finished treaty to Jefferson, recommending it be ratified by Congress. But Jefferson refused to send the treaty to the Senate for approval because it did not protect American sailors. Monroe was deeply insulted by Jefferson's action, and he blamed James Madison, now secretary of state, for helping to sink the treaty.

When he returned to the United States in 1807, he was determined to let Madison and Jefferson know how angry he was over the treaty. In 1808, he allowed his name to be put forward as a candidate for president against Madison. Madison easily won the election, and once more Monroe went back to Virginia.

Monroe returned to Virginia politics. He was elected to the Virginia Assembly in 1810, and began another term as governor in 1811. Soon afterward, President Madison asked Monroe to come to Washington and serve as his secretary of state. Monroe agreed and resigned as governor.

The War of 1812

When Monroe became secretary of state in March 1811, the relationship between Britain and the United States had broken down. The British practice of impressment continued to be a problem. Also, British officials in Canada were encouraging Native Americans to attack U.S. frontier settlements. Finally, in 1812, the conflict between Britain and the United States turned into a war.

Madison considered asking Monroe to lead troops in battle, but decided Monroe was too valuable as a member of the cabinet. He did ask Monroe to serve as acting secretary of war when Secretary William Eustis resigned. After Monroe held two major cabinet positions at the same time for two months, Madison appointed John Armstrong as the new war secretary.

The early months of the war went badly for the United States. They surrendered Fort Dearborn (now Chicago) and Detroit in the west, and two planned invasions of eastern Canada failed. During 1813, there was better news. Admiral Oliver Hazard Perry built a small fleet of warships on the banks of Lake Erie,

A portrait of James Monroe at about the time he served as secretary of state under President James Madison.

then used them to drive a British fleet into retreat. Soon afterward, General William Henry Harrison recaptured Detroit, then pursued the British occupiers into Canada, winning a major victory at the Thames River. Late in the year, American forces captured York (present-day Toronto, Ontario) and burned the Parliament House of Upper Canada, an act of destruction that the British would soon repay.

In 1814, as the Napoleonic Wars in Europe were ending, the British sent more ships and more troops to North America. In late summer, they landed in Maryland. They easily defeated an American force at Bladensburg, Maryland, where the Americans' panicky retreat was called "the Bladensburg Races." The British force continued directly to Washington, for which the new secretary of war had no plan of defense. Monroe even left his desk and led a *cavalry* unit to gain information on British troop movements, but the invaders could not be stopped.

As President Madison, Monroe, and other government leaders fled across the Potomac River into Virginia, the British entered Washington. There they set fire not only to the Capitol, but also to the Executive Mansion, the Library of Congress, and other government buildings.

Blame for the capture of Washington fell on Secretary of War Armstrong. Madison fired Armstrong and asked Monroe to take over as secretary of war once again. Monroe went to work immediately, helping to organize the defense of Baltimore, where the British were headed next. Three weeks after

The British captured Washington in August 1814 and set fire to the Capitol and other government buildings, including the Executive Mansion and the Library of Congress.

Washington had been occupied, American troops in Baltimore defeated the British. This American victory, together with another in northern New York,

The White House

The exterior of the Executive Mansion was made of sandstone, a stone that absorbs water and cracks easily. Even before the fire of 1814, workers covered the sandstone with whitewash, which soon chipped off. After the fire, they used 570 gallons of white paint to hide the cracks—and perhaps some places blackened by the fire. The mansion gradually became known as the White House. Years later, in 1901, President Theodore Roosevelt officially changed its name from the Executive Mansion to the White House.

☆ ☆ ☆

hastened negotiation of a treaty to end the war. In the meantime, Monroe served both as secretary of war and secretary of state.

The war was ended by the Treaty of Ghent, signed in December 1814. Neither the United States nor Britain had scored a clear victory. The war did prove to be a disaster for the Federalist Party in the United States. New England Federalists loudly opposed the war from the beginning, and they had even met to discuss seceding from the Union. Many Americans blamed them for holding back the U.S. war effort, and after 1815, the party gradually melted away.

Monroe's role in the war won him widespread admiration. His leadership had helped stop the British invasion after the attack on Washington. With the war over, a grateful nation turned its attention to the upcoming presidential election of 1816. After 40 years of service to his country, Monroe was finally considered the leading candidate for the nation's highest office.

The Star-Spangled Banner

The successful defense of Baltimore during the War of 1812 inspired Francis Scott Key to write the words to "The Star-Spangled Banner." Key was a Washington lawyer who was visiting the British fleet to arrange the release of an American prisoner. While he was on board a British ship, he witnessed the British bombardment of Fort McHenry at the entrance to Baltimore harbor on September 13 and 14, 1814. "By the dawn's early light," Key saw that the U.S. flag still flew from Fort McHenry. Fort McHenry and Baltimore had survived "the perilous fight." Inspired, Key immediately began writing verses about the event, and these later became the lyrics to "The Star-Spangled Banner." It became the official national anthem of the United States in 1931. The original Fort McHenry flag is on display at the National Museum of American History in Washington.

☆ ☆ ☆

Chapter 3

Nomination and Election ————————

To many, Monroe seemed the obvious choice to become the fifth president of the United States. His background was amazingly similar to those of the third and fourth presidents, Jefferson and Madison. Like Jefferson and Madison, Monroe was a Democratic-Republican, a Virginian, and a one-time secretary of state. He was as well prepared for the office as anyone could be.

Some observers, however, thought his background was a disadvantage. A Virginian had occupied the presidency for all but four years since the Constitution was ratified. They believed it was high time that leaders from other parts of the country gained the highest office.

Some Democratic-Republicans looked to William H. Crawford of Georgia as a candidate. Democratic-Republicans in Congress met

Virginians in the White House

Eight presidents have been born in Virginia, more than in any other state. Five remained residents of the state all their lives: George Washington, Thomas Jefferson, James Madison, James Monroe, and John Tyler. Three others—William Henry Harrison, Zachary Taylor, and Woodrow Wilson—moved to other regions as young men and made their political careers outside of Virginia.

☆ ☆ ☆

on March 16, 1816, to choose a candidate to represent the party in the presidential election. They voted to support Monroe, by a count of 65 to 54. As the party's candidate for vice president, they selected Daniel D. Tompkins, the governor of New York.

By winning the support of the Democratic-Republicans in Congress, Monroe took the most important step to the presidency. The opposition Federalist Party supported Rufus King of New York, but the Federalist Party was so weak that it was unable to mount a real challenge to Monroe. Neither candidate campaigned in the way that today's candidates do. It was considered impolite for candidates to trumpet their own candidacy. So candidates delivered no speeches and made no tours, leaving the campaigning to their supporters. However, even by these standards, the campaign of 1816 was calm, and there was little doubt about the outcome.

Monroe won a landslide victory. In the electoral college vote held in December 1816, Monroe won all but three states. He captured 183 votes to 34 votes for King, and became the fifth president of the United States. Tompkins was elected vice president.

Building a Cabinet

Even before final vote count was complete, Monroe was planning his administration. One of his first steps was to assemble his *cabinet*—the officials who help the president form national policy and manage federal departments. Monroe was determined to have each region of the nation represented in his cabinet. For secretary of state, he selected John Quincy Adams of Massachusetts. Adams had a long record of diplomatic service that was unmatched by anyone in the United States. As secretary of the treasury, Monroe chose his former presidential rival, Crawford of Georgia. Monroe hoped to select a western leader to head the war department, but he was unable to find a qualified westerner to accept the job. Finally, he chose John C. Calhoun of South Carolina.

Rounding out Monroe's cabinet were Secretary of the Navy Benjamin Crowninshield and Attorney General William Wirt. All but one of Monroe's original department heads would serve in his cabinet for the full eight years of his presidency. More than many presidents, Monroe valued the advice of his cabinet.

Monroe (standing) chose able men for his cabinet and relied on their advice. Secretary of State John Quincy Adams is at the left, and Secretary of War John C. Calhoun is on the right.

The Cabinet

In the 1700s, a small meeting room was called a cabinet. British kings met with their most trusted advisers in such a room, and the group was called the Council of the Cabinet. In the United States, the president's department heads came to be called simply the cabinet.

☆ ☆ ☆

He liked to read them drafts of speeches he had written, then rewrite the speech based on their comments. He made an effort not to play favorites or take sides in rivalries among cabinet officers.

The Inauguration

Monroe was sworn in as president on March 4, 1817. Just before noon, he and his wife left their private home in Washington and rode to the simple brick building where the U.S. Congress was meeting. (The Capitol was still being rebuilt after the British burned it in 1814.)

For the first time, the inauguration was held outdoors, not in the Congressional chambers. The ceremony was to be held in the House chambers, but Senators wanted to bring their own velvet-lined chairs over from the Senate

Monroe is sworn in as president by Chief Justice John Marshall, his old school friend, in an outdoor ceremony in 1817. The ruins of the Capitol, burned by the British in 1814, are in the background.

for the ceremony. The members of the House thought the senators were simply showing off, so they refused to let them bring their own chairs. As a compromise, the ceremony was held neither in the Senate nor in the House, but outdoors, setting a tradition that has continued ever since (except in very bad weather).

Nearly 8,000 people watched the inauguration. Monroe dressed in the earlier style of the Revolutionary era—black coat, knee breeches, ruffled scarf, and silk hose. Chief Justice John Marshall, Monroe's old school friend "Silver Heels," led Monroe in taking the presidential oath of office. Then Monroe delivered his inaugural address. He stressed the importance of improving the nation's defense and building more roads and canals. He also called for greater unity among people of differing political beliefs. The American people, he said, "constitute one great family with a common interest."

That evening, the Monroes attended a ball in their honor at the Davis Hotel. Afterward, they returned to their private home on I Street in Washington. Fire damage in the Executive Mansion was still being repaired, and it would not be ready for another six months. All over Washington, workers were repairing the damage done by the British during their occupation of the city in 1814.

The U.S. banking system was also still recovering from the war. The nation had run up a huge debt during the fighting and recovery. In 1816, one of James Madison's last acts as president was to revive the national bank, the Bank of the United States. Its opening was expected to help provide stability to the U.S. banking system. During Monroe's presidency, the nation's debt would become more manageable.

The United States in 1817 was more secure than it had ever been. Even though the War of 1812 had not been a clear victory, it earned the nation greater respect among the countries of the world. The United States enjoyed improved relations with Britain and with the other European powers. Perhaps for the first time in its history, the United States did not face a major crisis with the powerful nations of the world.

Much of the country's energy was focused on growth and expansion. The population of the United States grew to nearly 9 million in 1817—more than twice its population in 1790. Most importantly, waves of Americans kept moving west, settling in large numbers in the territories between the Appalachian

Mail for a Growing Nation

As the population of the United States grew, transportation and communication systems also expanded. For example, in 1789, there were just 75 post offices in the United States. In 1817, there were 3,459.

☆ ☆ ☆

Mountains and the Mississippi River. During Monroe's presidency, five new states would enter the Union—Mississippi, Illinois, Alabama, Maine (previously part of Massachusetts), and Missouri, the first state altogether west of the Mississippi.

Chapter 4

Grand Tour

Monroe began his presidency with a grand tour of the northern United States in 1817. He was following the example of George Washington, who had also toured the country at the start of his presidency. Like Washington, Monroe hoped to promote a sense of national unity and common purpose. The decline of the Federalist Party seemed to end a period of political bickering that had begun in the 1790s. Monroe's Democratic-Republicans were clearly in political control, and he wanted to show that he would be a leader for all Americans.

Monroe also had more practical reasons for making the trip. He wanted to inspect the nation's defenses. He had seen in the War of 1812 how easily the United States could be invaded. Now that there was little chance of a foreign invasion, it seemed an ideal time to prepare and improve the nation's defenses. Monroe hoped to build new forts to defend the nation's coasts, and new dockyards for the construction of warships. He also planned to improve defenses along the border with Canada. His tour would give him the chance to visit these areas and see them firsthand.

Monroe left Washington on June 1, 1817, traveling by horse-drawn carriage. Only his private secretary and General Joseph Swift traveled with him. At his first stop in Baltimore, the president was greeted by large crowds and banners, ringing bells and booming cannons. He visited Fort McHenry, where he gave a speech praising the people of Baltimore for the "glorious victory" won outside their city in the War of 1812.

The joyous welcome the president received in Baltimore was repeated at every stop he made. In Philadelphia, three troops of cavalry rode out to escort him into the city, where a huge crowd waited for him. In Trenton, New Jersey, he visited the Revolutionary War battlefield where he had been wounded 41 years earlier. Giving a brief speech there, he called the battlefield "the place where the hopes of the country were revived."

The greatest celebration of all was in Boston on the Fourth of July, where the president marked the national holiday by watching an exhibition of fireworks. During his stay, Monroe also climbed Bunker Hill, and attended a dinner hosted by John Adams, the former president and also the father of Monroe's secretary of state. Boston had long been a stronghold of the Federalist Party, but now the people of Boston rallied around the Democratic-Republican president. A reporter for a newspaper called the Boston *Columbian Centinel* commented on the new feeling of political unity in Boston and around the country. He wrote that Monroe's tour marked the beginning of an "era of good feelings" in the United States. The phrase was later widely used to describe the first years of the Monroe presidency.

Monroe began his journey by carriage, but he also often traveled by ship. He was the first president to make use of a new means of transportation, the steamship. Because they didn't depend on wind power and tides, steamships made travel faster and more predictable. By 1817, they were becoming widely used, and they were changing the way Americans traveled. Steamships were able to travel from New York to New Haven, Connecticut, in the record time of eight hours. On his tour, Monroe used steamships along the East Coast. He also traveled by steamship on the Hudson River to visit the United States Military Academy at West Point, New York.

Traveling by ship was a much more pleasant experience than traveling over the rough roads of 1817. At the time, many American roads were little more than dirt paths. They flooded after storms, and huge ruts could damage carriage wheels. Improving the nation's roads became a priority for Monroe. He also favored the building of canals to make travel by ship possible in the interior of the nation. The

An early steamboat on the Hudson River in New York. Monroe took a boat like this one up the river from New York City to the United States Military Academy at West Point, New York, during his tour of the northern states.

State of New York began building the Erie Canal, connecting Lake Erie to the Hudson River and the Atlantic Ocean, during Monroe's presidency.

In all, Monroe's tour covered 3,000 miles and lasted three and a half months. He returned to Washington on September 17, where he received one more welcoming salute. He was escorted into the city by cavalry and dignitaries on horseback.

The White House

Upon his return from the long tour, Monroe was finally able to move into the Executive Mansion. Workers had completed enough of the rebuilding to make the house livable, although work on the building would continue for years.

Monroe also introduced new rules of etiquette, or manners, for the White House. Under former presidents Jefferson and Madison, foreign diplomats could request a personal meeting with the president at any time. Because the workload of the office was increasing, Monroe required that diplomats meet first with the secretary of state or another cabinet official. This system was closer in style to the one used by European governments.

Monroe cut down on the number of parties and dinners hosted by the president. For years, congressmen and other Washington political figures had felt free to visit the White House at any time. Now, they were welcome to visit only when formally invited. Not surprisingly, these new rules bothered some people in Washington. They accused Monroe and the first lady of being snobs. To make matters worse, the first lady was often ill early in Monroe's presidency and failed to attend the important Washington parties. The exact nature of her illness has never been determined, but she may have suffered from epilepsy. Some of her critics called the first lady "Queen Elizabeth" because of her formal manner. Her older daughter Eliza sometimes served as hostess at the White House.

A grand public reception on New Year's Day 1818 helped soothe some of the hurt feelings. The reception celebrated the official reopening of the White House, and it was one of the biggest parties Washington had ever seen. Mrs. Monroe won high praise for her role as hostess and for her dazzling white gown from Paris.

Foreign Affairs

Many of the most urgent problems of Monroe's first term concerned the relationship between the United States and Spain. For hundreds of years, Spain had ruled colonies in Central America and South America. Spain still claimed large parts of the present-day United States, including Florida, Texas, New Mexico, Arizona, and California. In 1817, the boundaries between Spanish territory and United States territory were disputed.

Furnishing the White House

The Monroes had to pay for furniture, draperies, carpets, and other items needed in the White House. Some of their furniture is still on display there. The oval-shaped Blue Room is the best place to see the Monroes' taste in furniture. Armchairs, a bronze clock, and a marble-topped center table purchased by the Monroes in 1817 are still in use there. The Monroes ordered all their furniture from France.

These chairs, bought by James and Elizabeth Monroe for the White House, can still be seen there in the Blue Room.

☆ ★ ☆

Spanish-American relations were strained by difficulties in the then-Spanish province of Florida. Pirates were operating out of bases in Florida and attacking American merchant ships. The Seminole people who lived in Florida were raiding U.S. settlements in Georgia. Georgians also complained that the Seminole in Florida gave shelter to runaway slaves. The United States demanded that Spain control the pirates and impose rules on Native Americans in Florida.

The U.S. military commander in the south was Andrew Jackson of Tennessee. After a Seminole raid on a Georgia settlement, the government ordered Jackson to take a small force to Georgia to defend against the Seminole. If the Seminole withdrew to Florida, he had permission to pursue them.

Jackson chased the Native Americans into Florida—and then kept going. He captured Spanish forts at St. Mark's and Pensacola. He also captured two British citizens who he claimed were encouraging Seminole attacks, and executed them. Not surprisingly, both the Spanish and British ministers in Washington demanded an explanation from Monroe.

Monroe's cabinet was divided in its advice. Many members wanted to censure Andrew Jackson for his rash attacks and to apologize to Spain. Monroe and Secretary of State John Quincy Adams recognized that Jackson had gone too far, and they agreed to return the Spanish forts. However, they also tried to make Jackson's invasion work in favor of the United States. Jackson's easy capture of

Andrew Jackson, military commander in the south, chased Seminole raiders into Florida, where he captured two Spanish forts. His actions embarrassed Monroe's administration, but the following year, Spain sold the Florida Territory to the United States.

the forts shows that Spain clearly cannot control Florida, they said. To end the risk of other embarrassing incidents, they offered to buy the territory for $5 million. The Spanish agreed, and they also agreed to give up some disputed claims to the Oregon Territory and to parts of the old Louisiana Purchase.

Monroe and Adams had turned an embarrassing incident into a diplomatic victory. Spain and the United States signed the Adams-Onís (or Transcontinental) Treaty on February 22, 1819, adding Florida to the United States and setting borders between Spanish and U.S. territory all the way to the Pacific Ocean.

Two other important treaties were signed during Monroe's first term, both with Great Britain. The Rush-Bagot Treaty of 1817 reduced the number of warships the United States and Britain could deploy on the Great Lakes, reducing tensions between the United States and Canada (then still a British possession). The Convention of 1818 set the present border between the United States and Canada from Lake of the Woods, Minnesota, to the Rocky Mountains.

Monroe and Congress

Like all presidents, Monroe tried to establish a productive working relationship with members of Congress. At first glance, it seemed that the Era of Good Feelings would bring a smooth relationship. Monroe learned at second glance that the opposite was true. Since the Democratic-Republicans had no strong opposition, they did not have to vote together to keep control. They began breaking into factions and quarreling among themselves. Sometimes it seemed that the only thing Congress agreed about was that it should not follow the president's recommendations. As a result, Congress was able to exercise more power than ever before. In 1818, Justice Joseph Story observed, "The Executive has no longer a commanding influence."

As the president's power lessened, the House of Representatives rose in stature. Its Speaker, Henry Clay of Kentucky, supported a program of national economic development called the American System. It called for the federal government to pay for new and improved roads to link the eastern United States and the west. It also called for high *tariffs*, or taxes on imported goods. A tariff was designed to support American manufacturing by making foreign goods too expensive. The idea was that instead of buying expensive foreign products, Americans would buy affordable goods made in the United States.

Some of Clay's American System became law. A tariff on British cotton goods was raised in 1816, and a tariff on iron was raised in 1818. Plans for federally sponsored roads were more difficult, however. Many in Congress were opposed, and Monroe himself believed that the Constitution did not give the fed-

Henry Clay, Speaker of the House of Representatives, urged federal support for roads and canals, sometimes clashing with Monroe. In 1820, he helped fashion the Missouri Compromise, which brought a truce in arguments between northern and southern states.

eral government the power to build roads. He believed that road-building was the job of the individual states. The debate over who should pay for improvements to American transportation lasted throughout Monroe's presidency.

Fortunately, Congress was not in session for large parts of the year, leaving Monroe time for other things. He had been planning a second tour ever since returning from his first. In March 1819, Monroe embarked on a four-month tour that took him to most of the leading cities of the south and southwest. He traveled by steamboat to Norfolk, Virginia, then made his way to Charleston, South Carolina; Savannah and Augusta, Georgia; Nashville, Tennessee; and Lexington, Kentucky. The welcome he received on this tour was just as spectacular as on his first trip. He returned to the White House in August 1819.

The Panic of 1819

At stops all along the tour, Monroe often spoke of the continued prosperity of the United States. In fact, the nation was heading into a nationwide economic *depression* that became known as the Panic of 1819.

The panic had several causes. In the west, speculators had been borrowing large amounts of money from local banks to buy unsettled land from the government, hoping to sell it to new settlers for more than they paid. The paper money they borrowed was supposed to be backed up with gold, but local banks were printing more paper bills than they had gold for. The newly chartered Bank of the United States was lending money to the local banks. When it began demanding that local banks repay in gold—not in worthless paper bills—the local banks asked the speculators to repay their loans. The speculators asked settlers to repay their loans. When the settlers and speculators couldn't repay, local banks began closing, land prices fell, and a panic began.

In the east, merchants and traders were selling fewer products to Europe, which was recovering from 20 years of war. This led to a sharp drop in prices for wheat, cotton, and other agricultural products. Farmers could not sell their crops, and fewer ships filled with goods sailed for Europe, so sailors had no work. In Boston, 3,500 people were thrown in prison for not paying their debts. Another 1,800 were jailed in Philadelphia.

There was little Monroe could do to end the crisis. He did instruct the United States Treasury to give landowners more time to make payments on land

White House Wedding

On March 9, 1820, Monroe's younger daughter, Maria Hester Monroe, married Samuel L. Gouverneur. It was the first wedding ever performed at the White House. Only 42 family members and close friends were invited.

★ ★ ☆

bought from the federal government. In his message to Congress in 1819, he mentioned the large number of businesses closing. He urged Congress and the American people to support American manufacturing. However, the economic crisis did not let up until 1823.

Missouri

In the middle of the economic distress, another crisis arose. This crisis concerned slavery in Missouri, and it helped shape American politics for decades to come. The northern states, which had outlawed slavery, had a strong majority in the House of Representatives, where states receive representation according to their population. The north had more people and was growing more rapidly, leaving the south worried about its declining power. In the Senate, where each state has two representatives, the south had as many Senators as the north, and southerners wanted to keep it that way. To keep the balance between north and south in the Senate, southern senators insisted that states be admitted to the Union in pairs, one from the south and one from the north. Indiana was admitted in 1816, balanced by Mississippi in 1817. Illinois became a state in 1818, balanced by Alabama in 1819.

In 1818, Missouri applied for statehood. It was a difficult case. It was the first state completely west of the Mississippi River, where the issue of slavery had not yet been decided. In the House of Representatives, controlled by the north, Congressman James Tallmadge of New York argued that Missouri should join the Union only if it agreed to restrict slavery within its borders. Under the proposed Tallmadge amendment to the Missouri statehood bill, it would be illegal to bring new slaves into Missouri, and children of current slaves would be set free when they turned 25.

The amendment sparked an angry debate that divided the nation. Northerners supported Tallmadge's plan, and southerners angrily condemned it. If states west of the Mississippi were admitted to the Union as free states, the balance of power in the Senate would tip toward the antislavery north. If they were admitted as slave states, the balance would tip in favor of the proslavery south.

Tallmadge's plan left it up to Congress to decide whether Missouri and other new states would permit slavery. In contrast, Monroe and many Democratic-Republicans believed that Congress did not have the power to decide whether individual states should allow slavery or not. He believed that this was an issue for each state to decide for itself. The House passed the Tallmadge amendment in 1819, but southerners in the Senate made sure that it was not brought up for a vote.

Led by Speaker of the House Henry Clay, Congress finally arrived at a *compromise* and passed it in both the House and the Senate in April 1820. Under the compromise, Maine would be admitted as a free state immediately and Missouri would be admitted as a slave state when it organized a state government, balancing a northern and a southern state once again. The third element of the compromise set rules for other states to be admitted west of the Mississippi. It drew an east-west line at latitude 36° 30'—states north of the line would be free states, and those south of it would be slave states. Most congressmen north and south disliked this provision (for different reasons), but a majority voted in favor

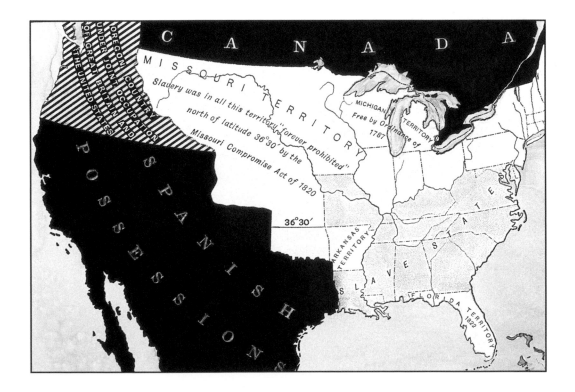

This map shows the main points in the Missouri Compromise. Missouri is admitted to the Union as a slave state, but slavery is prohibited in the remaining Missouri Territory north of the 36° 30' line (which runs along the southern border of Missouri).

to achieve the compromise. Monroe did not like the compromise either, but he also knew that the country might break into warring factions if he did not accept it. He signed the bill into law.

The Missouri Compromise was only a temporary solution. Secretary of State John Quincy Adams wrote that it was only "the title page to a great tragic volume." The debate over the spread of slavery would continue for another 40 years. During that time, the political divide between north and south would become deeper and deeper. Eventually, it led to the violent explosion of the Civil War.

Chapter 5

Running Unopposed ——————————

The Missouri Compromise shattered the political unity that the nation had been enjoying for several years. However, the disagreement over the compromise did not damage Monroe's standing among American voters. As his first term came to an end, there was no doubt that Monroe would be elected to serve a second term. In fact, not a single challenger stepped forward to run against him in the election of 1820. He was the first person since George Washington to run for president unopposed.

With only one candidate in the field, it is no surprise that the election was met with a lack of interest. Even in Monroe's home state of Virginia, only 4,321 of 600,000 voters showed up to vote. In the electoral college voting, Monroe won all but one electoral vote. A single elector—William Plumer of New Hampshire—voted for John Quincy Adams, who wasn't even running for president.

A portrait of James Monroe during his presidency, painted by Gilbert Stuart.

Monroe was sworn in for a second term as president on March 5, 1821. (The inauguration was to have been held on March 4. But since that date fell on a Sunday, the inauguration was delayed one day.) Dressed in formal black knee breeches and jacket, he took the oath of office in the overflowing chamber of the House of Representatives. The audience was so loud, and Monroe's speaking voice so soft, that few people heard his inaugural address. At the conclusion of the ceremony, he exited to cheers and to music played by the U.S. Marine Corps band. After the inauguration, the Monroes attended a ball at Brown's Hotel.

The Monroe Doctrine

Monroe's diplomacy with Spain in his first term had proved a spectacular success. In his second term, relations with Spain's former colonies would occupy much of his attention. By 1821, Spain's American empire was crumbling. That year, Mexico, Chile, Argentina, and Colombia all won their independence from Spain and were establishing themselves as new independent nations.

Many in Congress wanted to support the new republics. Like many Americans, they sympathized with South Americans' fight for independence from a colonial power, and their struggle reminded them of the American fight for independence almost 50 years earlier. They urged Monroe to formally recognize the republics' existence by exchanging diplomats with them.

The States During the Presidency of James Monroe

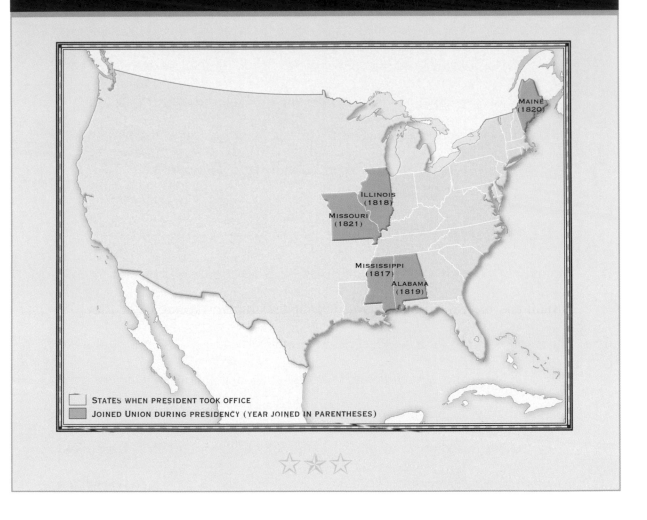

MAINE
(1820)

ILLINOIS
(1818)

MISSOURI
(1821)

MISSISSIPPI
(1817)

ALABAMA
(1819)

STATES WHEN PRESIDENT TOOK OFFICE
JOINED UNION DURING PRESIDENCY (YEAR JOINED IN PARENTHESES)

Monroe also sympathized with the new republics, but at first he saw no need to formally recognize them. He knew that doing so would only anger Spain. In 1817, Monroe decided to send special agents to South America to learn more about the situation there. Not until 1822 did he agree to exchange *diplomats* with Argentina, Colombia, and Chile, thereby formally recognizing the new republics.

Monroe was still concerned that European powers might help Spain recover her lost colonies. Rumors spread that a military expedition would be organized by France, Russia, Austria, and Prussia to crush the South American rebels. The prospect of European nations using force to maintain power in the Americas was alarming to Monroe. He searched for a way to warn the Europeans against military action. British diplomats offered a solution. They proposed that Britain and the United States issue a joint declaration warning other European nations against action in the Western Hemisphere.

Monroe and Secretary of State Adams worried that working with the British would make the United States look like a puny junior partner to Britain. They decided to set forth a separate American policy on the issue. On December 2, 1823, Monroe sent a statement to Congress that called for an end to European colonization in the Americas. Monroe wrote that the nations of North and South America were "free and independent" and "not to be considered as the subjects for future colonization by any European powers."

Simón Bolívar

The leader of the South American revolutions against Spain was Simón Bolívar. Born in Venezuela, he led wars of independence in his native country and in Colombia, Ecuador, Peru, and Bolivia. In the United States, Bolívar was sometimes called the George Washington of South America.

Simón Bolívar was a crusader for the independence of South American colonies from Spain. He was known as "the Liberator."

The policy statement later came to be known as the Monroe Doctrine, and it would prove to be Monroe's most significant action as president. The Monroe Doctrine's impact was mostly symbolic. Spain had little ability or intention to try to recover its lost South American colonies. In addition, if a unified group of European nations sent a military expedition, the United States did not have the military power to resist it. Still, the Monroe Doctrine announced to the world that the United States would demand the respect of other nations. It marked the first time that the United States asserted itself on equal terms with the other great nations of the world. It put the United States firmly on the side of democracy and self-government around the world.

Monroe won high praise for the policy statement. John J. Crittenden of Kentucky said that the message "has given us a more dignified and heroic attitude. It has made us the protector of the free governments of South America."

One target of the Monroe Doctrine was Russia, which claimed lands along the Pacific in the Oregon Territory, where it seemed interested in establishing a Russian colony. In 1824, the United States persuaded the Russians to give up their claims.

The American Colonization Society

Like many Americans, Monroe supported efforts to relocate African slaves from the United States to new homes in Africa. During his presidency, the American Colonization Society established a colony for freed African slaves in Liberia, in west Africa. They named the first settlement there Monrovia in his honor. Today Monrovia is the capital of Liberia.

☆ ☆ ☆

Monroe had less success with another diplomatic effort. He and Secretary of State John Quincy Adams negotiated a treaty with Great Britain that would stamp out the international slave trade. However, the U.S. Senate would approve only an amended version of the treaty that would limit the rights of other nations to search American ships. Great Britain rejected that change, and the treaty was lost. The chance to stamp out the slave trade slipped away.

Roads and Canals

One of the most hotly debated domestic issues of Monroe's second term was whether Congress had the power to fund new and improved roads and canals. Henry Clay urged the federal government to take the lead in making improvements to the transportation system. Early in Monroe's second term, Congress passed a bill authorizing repairs to the National Road, a crushed-stone highway that ran between Cumberland, Maryland, and Wheeling, Virginia (now West Virginia). Monroe recalled the longtime opposition of the old Democratic-Republicans to federal management of local projects. He vetoed the bill, insisting that it was up to the individual states to maintain the road. He maintained that the Constitution did not give Congress the power to collect tolls and make repairs on roads that it had not funded itself. It was the only time in his eight years as president that Monroe vetoed a measure passed by Congress.

Travelers on the National Road paid tolls to travel on it at tollhouses like this one. Monroe vetoed use of federal money to repair the road, which ran from Cumberland, Maryland, to Wheeling, Virginia (now West Virginia).

Still, Monroe knew that improving roads and canals was desperately needed. In 1824, Congress passed another bill that called for $30,000 to be spent on surveys for new roads and canals. Monroe signed this bill. On his last day in office, he signed another bill providing $150,000 to extend the National Road from Wheeling to Zanesville, Ohio. Most of the new construction of roads and canals during his presidency was paid for by states and private businesses, how-

Lafayette's Tour

In 1824, Monroe's old friend the Marquis de Lafayette toured the United States and visited every state of the Union. His tour came on the eve of the 50th anniversary of the American Revolution, in which Lafayette and Monroe served together. Lafayette was greeted throughout the United States as a hero of the Revolution.

The Marquis de Lafayette during his triumphal visit to America in 1824. He and Monroe had served together at Valley Forge in 1778, nearly 50 years earlier.

ever. During his term of office, the number of canals in the country increased from 100 to more than 1,000.

The Election of 1824

Monroe made it clear that he would follow the tradition of George Washington and other early presidents, retiring after his second term. Americans looked forward eagerly to the election of 1824, which came to be known as "the War of the Giants." Since all the candidates were considered members of his party, Monroe declined to support any candidate, leaving the choice up to the American people.

The leading candidates included three members of Monroe's cabinet: Secretary of War John C. Calhoun of South Carolina, Secretary of the Treasury William H. Crawford of Georgia, and Secretary of State John Quincy Adams of Massachusetts. The Congress produced two other strong candidates: House Speaker Henry Clay of Kentucky and Senator Andrew Jackson of Tennessee.

Jackson had more electoral votes than any other candidate, winning 99 votes, to 84 for Adams, 41 for Crawford, and 37 for Clay. Since he did not win a majority of the votes, however, the Constitution provided that the final choice would be made by the House of Representatives.

In the voting in the House, only the top three finishers could be candidates, with Speaker of the House Henry Clay eliminated from the field. Each state

John Quincy Adams, Monroe's secretary of state, became president in 1825 after a disputed election against Andrew Jackson.

delegation cast one vote. Clay threw his support to John Quincy Adams, and Adams won 13 of 24 votes, just one more than half, to gain the presidency. Soon afterward, he appointed Henry Clay his secretary of state. Jackson and his supporters were furious, believing that the election had been stolen from them by a "corrupt bargain" between Adams and Clay.

In his inauguration speech in March 1825, Adams heaped praise on Monroe for his achievements as president. Adams mentioned Monroe's skillful diplomatic efforts to acquire Florida. He noted that, thanks to Monroe, the nation's boundaries now extended to the Pacific Ocean. He praised Monroe's attention to improving the nation's coastal defenses and transportation systems. And he gave Monroe credit for trying to halt the international slave trade.

"The great features of [Monroe's] policy . . . have been to cherish peace while preparing for defensive war . . . and to proceed in the great system of internal improvements," Adams said.

Chapter 6

Worries

Monroe left the presidency with troubles weighing on his mind. His wife Eliza was so ill that the Monroes had to stay at the White House for several weeks after Adams's inauguration until she was well enough to travel.

Money troubles also worried Monroe. As a diplomat some 25 years earlier, his expenses were much greater than his diplomat's salary, and he paid the expenses out of his own pocket, falling deep into debt. Monroe intended to ask Congress to pay him back for those expenses but felt it was wrong to ask while he was still serving in the government. To raise some of the money he owed, Monroe sold part of his Virginia land.

When he left the presidency, he was still in debt, so he finally appealed to Congress to repay his expenses. Some in Congress hesitated to approve the payment, feeling that Monroe was asking for too much money. In 1826, Congress voted to repay Monroe nearly $30,000, considerably less than Monroe had hoped for.

Returning to Private Life

After leaving the White House, the Monroes moved to their estate in Leesburg, Virginia, called Oak Hill. Monroe supervised the planting of wheat and other grains, and the raising of sheep. The Monroes entertained visitors, including Lafayette and President Adams. Most of all, Monroe enjoyed being able once more to ride horses in the Virginia countryside, one of his favorite pastimes.

Monroe had little active involvement in politics after he left the presidency, but he kept in touch with his friends and associates in the government. He served as a member of the board of regents of the University of Virginia, which had been founded by Jefferson. In 1829, he served as president of the state convention called to create a new Virginia constitution. It was his last public service.

Eliza Monroe continued to suffer poor health. In 1826, she fell into a fireplace and suffered burns from which she never fully recovered. She died on September 23, 1830. Monroe was so shattered by his wife's death that he found it difficult to continue to live at Oak Hill. At the age of 72, he moved to New York City to live with his daughter Maria.

Oak Hill, the home in Virginia to which James and Elizabeth Monroe retired in 1825.

In Monroe's last years, he worked first on a book about the history of the world's governments, then on an autobiography. He was unable to complete either book. In spring 1831 he fell ill, and he died on July 4, 1831. He was the third of the first five presidents to die on that holiday. (Jefferson and John Adams had both died on July 4, 1826.)

Monroe's funeral in New York City was one of the largest the city had ever seen. Thousands of mourners lined the streets of New York. Bells rang and

After his death in New York City in 1831, James Monroe's body lay in state at City Hall.

guns fired in salute to the fallen president. Monroe was buried in New York, but in 1858 his coffin was moved and he was buried in his native Virginia.

Monroe's Legacy

Monroe was the last of the line of presidents from Virginia—Washington, Jefferson, Madison, and Monroe—who served for 32 of the first 36 years under the Constitution. Yet Monroe's presidency looked to the future more than it looked to the past. As president, he encouraged the nation's westward expansion and traveled west himself. By the time Monroe's presidency ended, one in four Americans lived west of the Appalachian Mountains. During his presidency, five new states joined the Union—Mississippi, Illinois, Alabama, Maine, and Missouri. Also during his presidency, the country gained claims to lands that extended all the way to the Pacific Ocean.

In 1858, Monroe's remains were carried back to Virginia. This is his tomb at Hollywood Cemetery in Richmond.

Monroe served at a time when congressional power began to overshadow the presidency. Like many presidents still to come, he found himself mostly powerless to take action against a serious economic depression. Monroe also was unable to play an important role on the crucial issues of slavery and states' rights, although he did sign the Missouri Compromise, which put off the threat of disunion and war for more than 30 years.

Above all, during Monroe's presidency, the United States became a more confident nation. The Monroe Doctrine was an expression of that new confidence. By warning European powers not to interfere with the independent nations of the Americas, Monroe placed the United States on equal footing with other great nations of the world. With the Monroe Doctrine, the United States for the first time displayed to the world the confidence and determination that would make it a world power in the years to come. The Monroe Doctrine is the best-remembered act of a presidency that saw the United States grow both in size and in prestige.

Fast Facts James Monroe

Birth:	April 28, 1758
Birthplace:	Westmoreland County, Virginia
Parents:	Spence and Elizabeth Jones Monroe
Brothers & Sisters:	Elizabeth Monroe Buckner (1754–?)
	Spence Monroe (1759–?)
	Andrew Monroe (1761?–1836)
	Joseph Jones Monroe (1764–1824)
Education:	College of William and Mary in Williamsburg, Virginia
Occupation:	Lawyer
Marriage:	To Elizabeth Kortright Monroe on February 16, 1786
Children:	Eliza Kortright Monroe Hay (1786–1840)
	(A son, born 1799, died in infancy)
	Maria Hester Monroe Gouverneur (1803–1850)
Political Party:	Democratic-Republican
Government Service:	1783–86 Member of the Confederation Congress
	1790–94 United States Senator from Virginia
	1794–96 U.S. Minister to France
	1799–1802 Governor of Virginia
	1803 Special Envoy to France
	1803–07 U.S. Minister to Great Britain
	1810–17 Secretary of State (under James Madison)
	1814–15 Secretary of War
	1817–25 Fifth President of the United States
His Vice President:	Daniel D. Tompkins (1774–1825)
Major Actions as President:	1818 Authorized General Andrew Jackson to pursue Seminole raiders into Florida
	1819 Approved treaty with Spain ceding Florida to the United States
	1823 Announced the Monroe Doctrine, warning other nations against interfering in the Americas
Firsts:	First president inaugurated in an outdoor ceremony
	First president to ride in a steamboat
	First (and only) president to have a foreign city named for him, Monrovia, in the new African state of Liberia
Death:	July 4, 1831 in New York, New York
Age at Death:	73
Burial Place:	Hollywood Cemetery, Richmond, Virginia

Fast Facts Elizabeth Kortright Monroe

Birth:	June 30, 1768
Birthplace:	New York, New York
Parents:	Lawrence and Hanna Aspinwall Kortright
Marriage:	To James Monroe, February 16, 1786
Children:	(*See* James Monroe at left)
Death:	September 23, 1830
Age at Death:	62 years
Burial Place:	Hollywood Cemetery, Richmond, Virginia

Timeline

1758	1774	1775	1776	1777–78
Born April 28 in Westmoreland County, Virginia	Father dies; Monroe enters College of William and Mary	Participates in raid on governor's mansion in Williamsburg to get arms for patriot militia	Joins Continental Army and is wounded at Battle of Trenton	Spends winter with Washington's army at Valley Forge

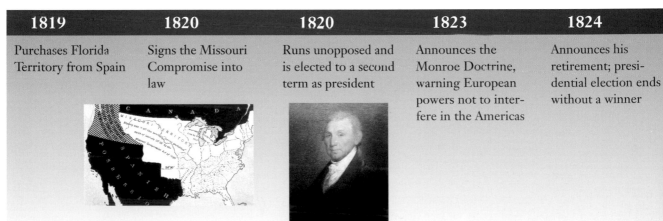

1794	1796	1799	1803	1807
Named minister to France by President George Washington	Dismissed as minister to France	Elected governor of Virginia	Helps negotiate Louisiana Purchase; appointed minister to Great Britain	Resigns as minister, returns home to Virginia

1819	1820	1820	1823	1824
Purchases Florida Territory from Spain	Signs the Missouri Compromise into law	Runs unopposed and is elected to a second term as president	Announces the Monroe Doctrine, warning European powers not to interfere in the Americas	Announces his retirement; presidential election ends without a winner

1782	1783	1786	1788	1790
Elected to Virginia House of Delegates	Elected to the Congress under the Articles of Confederation	Marries Elizabeth Kortright	Opposes ratification of Constitution by Virginia	Elected to the United States Senate

1810	1811	1814	1816	1817
Elected to Virginia Assembly	Appointed secretary of state by President James Madison	Named secretary of war by Madison, continuing as secretary of state	Elected president of the United States	Takes office as president March 4

1825	1829	1831
House of Representatives elects John Quincy Adams president; Monroe retires to Oak Hill estate in Virginia	Serves as president of Virginia state constitutional convention	Dies July 4 in New York City

Glossary

★ ★ ★ ★ ★

cabinet: a council advising a president or other chief executive

cavalry: part of a military force that operated on horseback

compromise: a settlement between two disagreeing sides in which each side agrees to give up something

depression: a period during which there is a severe decline in business; also called a panic

diplomat: a person who represents one country in negotiating with another country

impress: in naval history, to take a seaman prisoner and force him to work as a crewman on a ship of war

militia: citizen-soldiers called up in times of emergency

ratify: to formally approve

tariff: charges imposed by a government on imports

Further Reading

Kallen, Stuart. *John Marshall*. Edina, MN: Abdo Publishing, 2001.

Malone, Mary. *James Madison*. Springfield, NJ: Enslow Publishers, 1997.

Meltzer, Milton. *Thomas Jefferson: The Revolutionary Aristocrat*. New York: Franklin Watts, 1991.

Old, Wendie. *James Monroe*. Springfield, NJ: Enslow Publishers, 1998.

Santella, Andrew. *The War of 1812*. New York: Children's Press, 2001.

MORE ADVANCED READING

Ammon, Harry. *James Monroe: The Quest for National Identity*. New York: McGraw-Hill, 1971. Reprint, Charlottesville: University Press of Virginia, 1990.

Cresson, W. P. *James Monroe*. Chapel Hill: University of North Carolina Press, 1946.

Cunningham, Noble E. *The Presidency of James Monroe*. Lawrence: University Press of Kansas, 1996.

Dangerfield, George. *The Era of Good Feelings*. New York: Ivan Dee, 1989.

Elkins, Stanley, and Eric McKitrick. *The Age of Federalism*. New York: Oxford University Press, 1993.

Styron, Arthur. *Last of the Cocked Hats: James Monroe and the Virginia Dynasty*. Norman: University of Oklahoma Press, 1945.

Places to Visit

★ ★ ★ ★ ★

James Monroe Museum and Memorial Library

A museum with a large collection of Monroe artifacts and documents. The museum is operated by Mary Washington College.

908 Charles Street
Fredericksburg, Virginia 22401
(540) 654-1043
http://jamesmonroemuseum.mwc.edu

Ash Lawn-Highland

One of James Monroe's Virginia homes.

1000 James Monroe Parkway
Charlottesville, Virginia 22902
(434) 293-9539
http://monticello.avenue.org/ashlawn

National Museum of American History

A museum of the Smithsonian Institution where the original Star-spangled Banner is preserved.

14th Street and Constitution Avenue, NW
Washington, D.C.
(201) 357-2700
http://www.americanhistory.si.edu

Valley Forge National Historic Park

Site of the winter camp where young James Monroe and the rest of the Continental Army survived bitter cold and low rations.

Route 23 and N. Gulph Road
P.O. Box 953
Valley Forge, Pennsylvania 19482
(610) 783-1077
http://www.nps.gov/vafo/index.htm

Online Sites of Interest

★ **The American President**

http://www.americanpresident.org

Biographies of Monroe and all the other presidents of the United States.

★ **Internet Public Library, Presidents of the United States (IPL POTUS)**

http://www.ipl.org/POTUS/

An excellent resource for personal, political, and historical materials about each president. It includes links to other Internet sites.

★ **The White House**

http://www.whitehouse.gov/history/presidents/jm5.html

A short biography from the White House.

★ **Grolier Online: The American Presidents**

http://gi.grolier.com/presidents/

Biographies of the presidents at different reading levels from Grolier encyclopedias.

★ **Presidents USA**

http://www.presidentsusa.net/monroe.html

Provides excellent links to other Monroe sites, including the texts of his inaugural addresses.

★ **James Monroe's Land Holdings**

http://etext.lib.virginia.edu/users/fennell/highland/

An interesting history of the various residents and plantations Monroe owned during his life.

★ **Portraits and Letters of James Monroe**

http://www.swem.wm.edu/spcoll/Monroe/monroemain.htm

Items from the special collections of the Swem Library at the College of William and Mary, including portraits of Monroe, letters in his own hand, and other documents.

For other online sites, *see* "Places to Visit."

Table of Presidents

	1. George Washington	**2. John Adams**	**3. Thomas Jefferson**	**4. James Madison**
Took office	Apr 30 1789	Mar 4 1797	Mar 4 1801	Mar 4 1809
Left office	Mar 3 1797	Mar 3 1801	Mar 3 1809	Mar 3 1817
Birthplace	Westmoreland Co, VA	Braintree, MA	Shadwell, VA	Port Conway, VA
Birth date	Feb 22 1732	Oct 20 1735	Apr 13 1743	Mar 16 1751
Death date	Dec 14 1799	July 4 1826	July 4 1826	June 28 1836

  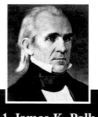 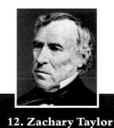

	9. William H. Harrison	**10. John Tyler**	**11. James K. Polk**	**12. Zachary Taylor**
Took office	Mar 4 1841	Apr 6 1841	Mar 4 1845	Mar 5 1849
Left office	**Apr 4 1841•**	Mar 3 1845	Mar 3 1849	**July 9 1850•**
Birthplace	Berkeley, VA	Greenway, VA	Mecklenburg Co, NC	Barboursville, VA
Birth date	Feb 9 1773	Mar 29 1790	Nov 2 1795	Nov 24 1784
Death date	Apr 4 1841	Jan 18 1862	June 15 1849	July 9 1850

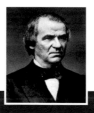   

	17. Andrew Johnson	**18. Ulysses S. Grant**	**19. Rutherford B. Hayes**	**20. James A. Garfield**
Took office	Apr 15 1865	Mar 4 1869	Mar 4 1877	Mar 4 1881
Left office	Mar 3 1869	Mar 3 1877	Mar 3 1881	**Sept 19 1881•**
Birthplace	Raleigh, NC	Point Pleasant, OH	Delaware, OH	Orange, OH
Birth date	Dec 29 1808	Apr 27 1822	Oct 4 1822	Nov 19 1831
Death date	July 31 1875	July 23 1885	Jan 17 1893	Sept 19 1881

5. James Monroe

6. John Quincy Adams

7. Andrew Jackson

8. Martin Van Buren

Mar 4 1817	Mar 4 1825	Mar 4 1829	Mar 4 1837
Mar 3 1825	Mar 3 1829	Mar 3 1837	Mar 3 1841
Westmoreland Co, VA	Braintree, MA	The Waxhaws, SC	Kinderhook, NY
Apr 28 1758	July 11 1767	Mar 15 1767	Dec 5 1782
July 4 1831	Feb 23 1848	June 8 1845	July 24 1862

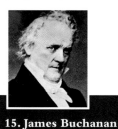

13. Millard Fillmore

14. Franklin Pierce

15. James Buchanan

16. Abraham Lincoln

July 9 1850	Mar 4 1853	Mar 4 1857	Mar 4 1861
Mar 3 1853	Mar 3 1857	Mar 3 1861	**Apr 15 1865•**
Locke Township, NY	Hillsborough, NH	Cove Gap, PA	Hardin Co, KY
Jan 7 1800	Nov 23 1804	Apr 23 1791	Feb 12 1809
Mar 8 1874	Oct 8 1869	June 1 1868	Apr 15 1865

21. Chester A. Arthur

22. Grover Cleveland

23. Benjamin Harrison

24. Grover Cleveland

Sept 19 1881	Mar 4 1885	Mar 4 1889	Mar 4 1893
Mar 3 1885	Mar 3 1889	Mar 3 1893	Mar 3 1897
Fairfield, VT	Caldwell, NJ	North Bend, OH	Caldwell, NJ
Oct 5 1830	Mar 18 1837	Aug 20 1833	Mar 18 1837
Nov 18 1886	June 24 1908	Mar 13 1901	June 24 1908

25. William McKinley **26. Theodore Roosevelt** **27. William H. Taft** **28. Woodrow Wilson**

	25. William McKinley	26. Theodore Roosevelt	27. William H. Taft	28. Woodrow Wilson
Took office	Mar 4 1897	Sept 14 1901	Mar 4 1909	Mar 4 1913
Left office	**Sept 14 1901•**	Mar 3 1909	Mar 3 1913	Mar 3 1921
Birthplace	Niles, OH	New York, NY	Cincinnati, OH	Staunton, VA
Birth date	Jan 29 1843	Oct 27 1858	Sept 15 1857	Dec 28 1856
Death date	Sept 14 1901	Jan 6 1919	Mar 8 1930	Feb 3 1924

33. Harry S. Truman **34. Dwight D. Eisenhower** **35. John F. Kennedy** **36. Lyndon B. Johnson**

	33. Harry S. Truman	34. Dwight D. Eisenhower	35. John F. Kennedy	36. Lyndon B. Johnson
Took office	Apr 12 1945	Jan 20 1953	Jan 20 1961	Nov 22 1963
Left office	Jan 20 1953	Jan 20 1961	**Nov 22 1963•**	Jan 20 1969
Birthplace	Lamar, MO	Denison, TX	Brookline, MA	Johnson City, TX
Birth date	May 8 1884	Oct 14 1890	May 29 1917	Aug 27 1908
Death date	Dec 26 1972	Mar 28 1969	Nov 22 1963	Jan 22 1973

41. George Bush **42. Bill Clinton** **43. George W. Bush**

	41. George Bush	42. Bill Clinton	43. George W. Bush	
Took office	Jan 20 1989	Jan 20 1993	Jan 20 2001	
Left office	Jan 20 1993	Jan 20 2001	—	
Birthplace	Milton, MA	Hope, AR	New Haven, CT	
Birth date	June 12 1924	Aug 19 1946	July 6 1946	
Death date	—	—	—	

29. Warren G. Harding	**30. Calvin Coolidge**	**31. Herbert Hoover**	**32. Franklin D. Roosevelt**
Mar 4 1921	Aug 2 1923	Mar 4 1929	Mar 4 1933
Aug 2 1923•	Mar 3 1929	Mar 3 1933	**Apr 12 1945•**
Blooming Grove, OH	Plymouth, VT	West Branch, IA	Hyde Park, NY
Nov 21 1865	July 4 1872	Aug 10 1874	Jan 30 1882
Aug 2 1923	Jan 5 1933	Oct 20 1964	Apr 12 1945

37. Richard M. Nixon	**38. Gerald R. Ford**	**39. Jimmy Carter**	**40. Ronald Reagan**
Jan 20 1969	Aug 9 1974	Jan 20 1977	Jan 20 1981
Aug 9 1974★	Jan 20 1977	Jan 20 1981	Jan 20 1989
Yorba Linda, CA	Omaha, NE	Plains, GA	Tampico, IL
Jan 9 1913	July 14 1913	Oct 1 1924	Feb 11 1911
Apr 22 1994	—	—	—

• Indicates the president died while in office.

★ Richard Nixon resigned before his term expired.

Index

Page numbers in *italics* indicate illustrations.

About the Author

Andrew Santella writes magazine articles and book reviews. His work has appeared in the *New York Times Book Review*, *GQ*, *Commonweal*, and other publications. He is the author of a number of nonfiction books for young readers, including *The War of 1812*. He lives outside Chicago and is a graduate of Loyola University.